I0126518

ANALYSIS OF

PROFESSIONAL TRAINING EFFECTIVENESS

FOR THE SPA MANAGER ROLE IN ITALY:

ADDRESSING MARKET GAPS

OAXIES® PUBLISHING SPA RESEARCH SERIES

Simone Esposito, BSc

ANALYSIS OF

PROFESSIONAL TRAINING EFFECTIVENESS

FOR THE SPA MANAGER ROLE IN ITALY:

ADDRESSING MARKET GAPS

OaXIES
PUBLISHING

OAXIES® PUBLISHING SPA RESEARCH SERIES

Simone Esposito, BSc | s.esposito@oaxies.com

ANALYSIS OF
PROFESSIONAL TRAINING EFFECTIVENESS
FOR THE SPA MANAGER ROLE IN ITALY:
ADDRESSING MARKET GAPS

Published by OAXIES® LTD
Roseneath, 4 Hardwick Mount, Buxton SK17 6PP, UK
http://www.oaxies.com | info@oaxies.com

OAXIES® LTD is a company registered in England and Wales
Company Number: 10233754

OAXIES® is a trademark registered in the EU
Trademark Number: 016025595

ISBN-13: 978-1-9998205-0-3
ISBN-10: 1-99-982050-9

1st Edition, Copyright © 2018 by OAXIES® LTD

All rights reserved. The text of this publication, or any part thereof, many not be reproduced or transmitted in any form or by any means, electronic or mechanical, including photocopying, recording, storage in an retrieval system, or otherwise, without prior permission of the publisher.

All trademarks used herein are the property of their respective owners. The use of trademarks or brand names in this text does not imply any affiliation with or endorsement of this book by such owners.

Copy Editing by Ilaria Poluzzi | i.poluzzi@oaxies.com
Cover Photo and Graphic Design by Simone Esposito | s.esposito@oaxies.com

Printed by CreateSpace, An Amazon.com Company

TABLE OF CONTENTS

© 2018 OAXIES® LTD

LIST OF TABLES

LIST OF FIGURES

© 2018 OAXIES® LTD

AUTHOR

Simone Esposito, BSc

After the BSc (Hons) International Spa Management at the University of Derby, he is currently achieving the homonymous MSc.

Beauty Therapist, specialised in massage and spa treatments, has worked in Italy and England covering different roles in the Beauty & Spa Industry.

With Ilaria Poluzzi he has founded the brand Oaxies®, a start-up company specialised in spa maagement, with headquarter based in Buxton, UK.

ACKNOWLEDGMENTS

For the realisation of this dream come true, which I could never have imagined possible and which is the result of years of sacrifice in an initially foreign country but then became a home, I want to thank first of all my family, which has always supported me in every way possible; my partner Ilaria, to whom I owe so much for always being close and finally, but more importantly, I would like to thank my daughter Sally Sophie who through her smile gives me the strength to go beyond my expectations.

Thanks also to my supervisor Dr. Iride Azara for the support and to the University of Derby Buxton Campus, where together with my colleagues from simple spectators we have conquered the role of actors, being able to give a new shape to our life.

© 2018 OAXIES® LTD

ABSTRACT

This study aims to investigate the effectiveness of Italian spa management professional training, taking into account current educational system and programmes.

In doing so the objectives of this research are to analyse the current training and educational systems programmes world-wide and in Italy, as effective routes to spa managerial positions and employment; to analyse the skills and attributes required to operates as a spa manager in Italy and at international level; to evaluate the competitiveness, barriers and opportunities of the Italian spa industry in relation to recruiting effective, competent and talented spa manager; give recommendations for improving and implementing the Italian spa management educational and training system.

A qualitatively oriented study in the form of a comparative case study design, with an inductive approach, has been chosen. The authors have deployed 19 semi-structured interviews and questionnaires, and questionnaires have been deployed to Italian or working in Italy spa managers (11), spa directors (2), industry leaders such as association presidents (2), consultants (2), trainers (1) and representative of trade associations (1); giving them the chance to explain their opinions on the importance of basic qualifications and experiences, the current educational system and the management skills for spa the industry. The sampling strategy procedure is purposive, each interviewed was selected following certain criteria like the type of role, position and experience in the industry, knowledge of the topic.

Key findings shows there is the need in Italy for a specific path for spa management educational programmes. Indeed, as stated by Global Spa and Wellness Summit (2012), nowadays there are only a few and the existing ones are seen as weak in preparing students for the workplace. The gaps in the Italian education and training system for spa management that must be overcome, identified as barriers for its development, are the obsolescence of Italian regulations and laws, in particular Italian Law Reordering the Thermal Spa Sector Law no. 323/2000 and Discipline of the Beautician Activity Law no. 1/1990, but there is the willingness from representatives of trade associations and training associations, aware of the need to change and expand the law in order to make changes, on working on it to improve the current spa management educational and training system, hand in hand with the change and adaptation of regulations. Also, the costs for labor, the high salary for managers and lack of investments in the sector has been recognised as the most important barriers. Despite most respondents are unaware of the education and training system in other countries, also representatives of training and trade associations, the current status of Italian training and educational systems for spa manager has been described unsatisfactory, superficial, defective and incomplete. Moreover, the interviewed could not recognise a benchmarking or competitiveness of Italian spa management educational system but only dissatisfaction and backwardness, pointing out both the lack and the need of recognition of the role, at educational and profession level, and of a specific spa management path, which clearly create a gap in the system.

The analysis highlighted that the career for the most totality of interviewed has been in hospitality or in the beauty industry and for a minority in the fitness & wellness industry because, as stated by Rossi (2015) the work experience in hotels, in departments such as front office or public relations, can be helpful to facilitates the relationship with other departments and customers as well (Rossi, 2015). While the training undertaken has been mainly in beauty and complimentary therapy or academic degree plus some specialisation courses. Confirming the survey conducted for the Global Spa & Wellness Summit (GSWS,

© 2018 OAXIES® LTD

2012) stating that the industry relevance to educational qualifications when recruiting managers is little because the working
experience in the management and spa sector is most important
professional qualifications, followed by the importance of training or experience in spa, the experience has been deemed more
important than education and training but has been difficult to
determine the minimum amount of years needed.

Solutions and suggestions for improvement have been identified in the enlargement and adaptation of existing programmes,
more structured and detailed with focus on marketing, business
and human resources; and the implementation of an internship in
the spa environment to learn the job.

1 INTRODUCTION

In recent years, the spa industry has grown rapidly throughout Europe, which has led to an associated increase in the demand for education in spa management. Academic resources related to spa management are very limited and most of the literature consists of reports, conference proceedings and commercial articles. The published spa research is still very little in Finland, where the most listed companies are dealing with spa as part of the broader concept of tourism for health and well-being. The most advanced in the research are the German-speaking countries (Austria, Germany, Switzerland), where some surveys have been carried out on the management of the spas, examining the level of education of the spa managers and the spa staff. In Spain, the ILIS project carried out a research taking into consideration the spa managers and their staff. UK resources also present mostly spa and market data with a gap in spa management, with the exception of academic manuals. A similar lack of literature in the field of spa management has been observed in Italy and Poland, with only a few articles and books on related subject (Bielanski et al., 2011).

Investigating the shortcomings in this market and the fundamental skills for a spa manager is important. Indeed, the challenge that spa companies are facing, linked to managerial positions, is serious because there are not enough competent people to hold management positions (GSWS, 2012). In order to work in the spa sector one must have a great predisposition to human contact, be open, extroverted, creative and selfless. Furthermore, being constantly on the rise and always ready to enrich their cultural background (Virgintino & Bovero, 2013). "Learning is

© 2018 OAXIES® LTD

the process of acquisition, integration and interpretation of new knowledge with the aim of a subsequent use" as stated by Casillas et al. (2010, p.163).

The ability to renew knowledge, create new ideas and be innovative are key features for the spa. It is then necessary a workforce with more abilities, competences and problem-solving skills (Rawlinson & Heap, 2017).

1.1 AIM AND OBJECTIVES

It follows, the aim of this research is to investigate the effectiveness of professional training for the Spa manager role in Italy, taking into account current educational system and programmes.

The objectives of this study are:

1. Analyse the current training and educational systems programmes worldwide and in Italy, as effective routes to spa managerial positions and employment;

2. Analyse the skills and attributes required to operates as a spa manager in Italy and at international level;

3. Evaluate the competitiveness, barriers and opportunities of the Italian spa industry in relation to recruiting effective, competent and talented spa managers;

4. Recommendations for improving and implementing the Italian spa management educational and training system.

In doing so, the research question is: what are the gaps in the Italian education system that must be overcome?

© 2018 OAXIES® LTD

2 LITERATURE REVIEW

2.1 THE GLOBAL SPA INDUSTRY

The spa sector has grown considerably in recent years, with a value of 60.3 billion dollars a year according to the Global Spa Summit (2010). The forecasts for the future of the spa industry are for development and expansion; the global spa market will have a value of 77.2 billion US dollars by 2015, according to a study conducted by Global Industry Analysts (GIA).

In Europe there is the presence of more than 1,400 medically respected health and medical spas (ESPA, 2018), providers of physical care to those who are usually called patients. The Global Wellness Institute (2014), has drawn up a top 20 in which the majority of countries with ancient tradition of mineral springs and the existence of numerous spas, sanatoriums and balneotherapy are European. Most of Eastern Europe and the Baltic countries, including Germany, Austria, Switzerland, Italy, have a long 'kur' tradition, in curative, rehabilitative and preventive therapy (GWI, 2014; Frost, 2004).

The concept of wellness is subject to different interpretations (Cohen & Bodecker, 2008; Foster & Keller, 2008; Smith & Kelly, 2006) although currently the term spa is used indifferently all over the world, whether there are thermal springs or not (Altman, 2000). It is based on the holistic and natural approach to the health and treatment of various disorders, using mineral thermal waters from sources at different temperatures.

Health and wellness have recently become similar terms, but it is good to remember that health concerns the medical or curative aspects, while wellness concerns more the preventive ones (Smith & Puczko, 2014). The birth of the revisited concept takes place between the nineteenth and the twenty-first century, with the aim of preventing diseases through the promotion of informed health, education and a holistic approach to nutrition, with a view to both mental and spiritual balance (Cohen & Bodecker, 2008; IUTO, 1973). Later, a new type of spa was developed, in which the healing aspect of mineral waters goes hand in hand with wellness treatments, including the medical and wellness side of the treatments.

2.1.1 HEALTH VERSUS WELLNESS

As already mentioned, the terms health and wellness have a conceptually different meaning depending on the country and culture. In Central and Eastern Europe and the Baltic States, it is linked to treatments that tend to be curative for certain physical conditions, along with medical advice and doctor supervision. In fact, given the presence of medical waters, the term health is associated with the therapeutic medical and physical healing concept. These historic medical spas are characterised by the presence of a doctor who oversees the treatment provided, based on a prescription from the practitioner, since the natural and medical waters are used for specific conditions such as mobility problems or circulatory disorders. This is why in Europe the term 'spa' means different things given by the traditional presence of water based treatments and wet areas. Unlike Western Europe, in particular the Atlantic coast, familiar to the thalassotherapy concept, in the USA or the United Kingdom hydrotherapy or balneotherapy are unknown concepts more related to wellness, since they might not involve water as accustomed to beauty salons. Finding a clinical environment in these baths or medical sanatoriums, often translated as a spa, would be a surprise (Smith & Puczko, 2014).

The water properties are recognised, receiving government support and regulation, in many European countries, with health reimbursements provided by health insurance, at least in part, for

© 2018 OAXIES® LTD

treatments. In contrast, no medical specialisation is recognised in the United Kingdom, the Netherlands, Sweden, and Denmark (Gutenbrunner et al., 2010; Buxton, 2017).

2.2 THE ROLE OF EDUCATION AND TRAINING IN THE PROFESSIONALISATION OF SPA WORKFORCE

Nowadays, spas are described as "places dedicated to overall well-being through a variety of professional services that promote the renewal of mind, body and spirit" (ISPA, 2017) but there is the perception of a lack of qualified and experienced managers, in order to satisfy the growth of demand. This lack of spa managers and even management training have been identified as the main obstacles to the successful growth of spa companies worldwide (Rawlinson, 2018). Furthermore, the skills required by spa managers have been fragmented and complicated by the evolution, growth and globalisation of the industry, and they vary considerably depending on the location, type and size of the spa. Business acumen, leadership, financial understanding, people connection, experience and practical practitioner skill and an understanding of spa philosophy are the basis of the skills gaps for these global spa managers, as discovered by Dowthwaite (2012; Dowthwaite & Rawlinson, 2018).

The characteristics to become a spa manager are certainly the all-round passion for the wellness sector. Basic knowledge of aesthetics, cosmetics and a genuine curiosity towards the news of the sector are also necessary, as well as patience and a collaborative temperament to manage a 10-15 people staff. Participate to conferences, visiting spas, discovering new products and massage techniques is also important (Rossi, 2015).

The management of schedules and requests for appointments, the assessment of the status of inventories, the study of products and finally the development of new promotional and marketing ideas to engage customers are part of the daily activities. The management of the structure at the technical level, knowing every benefit and contraindication of the offered treatments, the market flows, the type of clientele and the habits of the territory are necessary abilities. The work experience at the hotel, in departments such as front office or public relations, can therefore be favourable since the general functioning of the hotels facilitates the relationship with the other departments and with the customers (Rossi, 2015). Often the hotel spas (ISPA, 2017) erroneously choose a competent beautician but without knowledge of hospitality (Rossi, 2015).

In a research conducted by Bielanski et al., it was indicated by managers that the main tasks are sales and marketing. Furthermore, in all the countries analysed (Austria, Spain, Finland, Poland, Great Britain) a manager was responsible for 6 main tasks and the assigned ones were: finances, human resources, strategic planning and rarely, but not less important, customer service policy and quality management. Majority of the managers (91%) had a higher education, in particular Masters degree (59%), Bachelor's degree (32%) and higher vocational education (9%). More than 50% had over 6 years of work experience in spa centre management and 30% have worked between 1 and 3 years in the field. In addition, over 50% of spa managers have been previously trained in: leadership, IT and quality control (Bielanski et al., 2011).

The average importance of skills was statistically significantly higher for managers than for their staff and the importance of skills for managers was significantly higher than their need for training (Bielanski et al., 2011).

The figure of the spa manager is very complex compared to a business manager. It is important to know how to lead a group, being able to do what is required of the employees, both in qualitative and quantitative terms, being recognised as a leader but relating with a superior to communicate action plans and results, knowing how to set up effective procedures and methods to be respected, defining policies to guarantee control and continuous development, which are all essential skills (Minardi, 2017). At the same time, it is necessary to know how to define and achieve the objectives, developing a clear global vision of the business

© 2018 OAXIES® LTD

plan and related commercial communication strategies. Identify, select, manage and motivate staff members by personally setting up and developing training plans is also mandatory. For this reason, the role can not be assigned lightly or in a casual way, being the basis for the creation and maintenance of a successful business within the spa (Minardi, 2017).

The Global Spa & Wellness Summit (GSWS, 2012) has conducted a survey were both industry executive/leaders and spa managers/directors have expressed on the importance of different qualifications and basic experiences for a spa manager position. Management or spa industry working experience has been recognised as the most important professional qualifications, followed by the importance spa training or experience. Formal educational credentials have been considered only moderately important by the majority. The reasons are different: firstly, there are currently a limited number of specific educational programs for spa management and, secondly, the existing ones are seen as somewhat distant from the needs of the industry and weak in the preparation of the students to the work place. Most of them have indicated their preference to hire a manager or a manager with a relevant degree, in case of equality between the factors, but given limited availability of them, they can not be picky. One of the biggest challenges for spas has indeed been identified in training and education, as well as the lack of well trained personnel (GSWS, 2012).

According to Bielanski et al. (2011) managers are willing to be further trained not only in strictly managerial skills, but also in operational skills, stating that staff should be trained in managerial skills such as: quality management, sales, marketing. Presumably therefore, nowadays managers expect that the staff is not only professionally trained on treatments, but also customer-oriented and aware of quality policies.

The GSWS report (2012) states that the industry give little relevance to educational qualifications when recruiting managers, and this is one of the key factors contributing to the business sector skills gap (Rawlison, 2017).

According to Cohen and Bodecker (2008) spa managers often come from therapist positions, being currently the highest position for them the role of treatment manager, acting as a springboard for spa management. Managers and leaders generally deals with product development, human resource management, marketing and business development and the financial aspects of the business. Management roles can be generic or specialist and spa management career paths generally start with Assistant Spa Manager leading to Spa Manager and Spa Director. Further job titles, depending on the scope and responsibilities, include Spa Operations Manager, Spa Business Development Manager, Director of Wellness or Group Spa Director (Cohen & Bodecker, 2008).

There are few schools worldwide that offer graduation programs related to spa management, and existing programs are relatively new and relatively small, and because of this the stakeholders in the spa sector generally have little awareness of it, but also because of the lack of interaction and collaboration between the spa industry and schools. There are also around 64 universities, colleges and schools all over the world that currently offer degrees in or are associated to spa management. Over three quarters of these schools are located in North America and Europe, with only a small handful in other regions of the world. In fact, 41% of schools are in only two countries, the United States and the United Kingdom (GSWS, 2012).

Most schools offer Bachelor's degrees of 3/4 years or Foundation or Associate degree of 2 years. Just under half of the schools offer "pure" spa management programs such as "Resort and spa management" or "Salon and spa management" and only 10 schools of hotel, hospitality, tourism, resort, business management, or similar, have a formal concentration in spa management, while a slightly higher number of these have 1 or 3 optional courses relating to the spa. Moreover, 16 schools offers spa/beauty therapy or aesthetics degree combined with business/ management training (GSWS, 2012). There are three different types of programmes:
• Pure spa management programmes: preparation focused on

   © 2018 OAXIES® LTD

spa management career, seen as the most ideal preparation for spa managers/directors as they provide the most targeted and relevant curriculum. 27 universities/colleges/schools world-wide offer these kinds of degrees, primarily located in Europe (14 schools) and North America (9 schools). All degree levels: Master's (6 schools), Bachelor's (6 schools), Foundation/Associate's (16 schools), and Certificate/Diploma (9 schools). The focus is on both management and business related topics as well as on spa and wellness related topics. Ideally, they should include practical work experience component   which may not be enough to skip a recent graduate directly to the spa manager position, with a high level of responsibility. Therefore, unless a student already has previous work experience before, which is relatively rare, a position of assistant manager at a lower level would probably be the best option, with the opportunity to quickly advance as job experience and practical skills are acquired (GSWS, 2012);

- Spa management track or spa management electives as part of broader degree programmes in small number of schools that offer degrees in hospitality, hotel, tourism, resort management and business management. There are about 22 schools world-wide, mainly in North America (10 schools) and Asia-Pacific (7 schools), most of them at Bachelor's degree level, ranging from just 1 or 2 elective courses on spa to a more formalised and extensive spa management concentration or area of emphasis, typically an addition to the curricula of Hospitality, Hotel, Tourism, Resort, Business Management degree programmes. Most programmes of this nature have a broad and well-defined curriculum of study on a range of technical subjects as well as specific subjects to the sector. The strengths of these kinds of programmes is that their graduates gain a very rigorous education in all the technical skills that are required to be a good manager. Arguably, graduates of these programmes may be the best prepared in terms of hard skills and technical management knowledge. Additionally, they gain a well-rounded skill set that prepares them for work across a range of possible jobs; for that reason they have the opportunity to advance their careers by moving between positions in the spa and hospitality, hotel sectors with greater opportunity to move into a higher-level management (GSWS, 2012);

- Spa therapy combined with spa management component, offered in a growing number of schools, with training in spa therapies and the addition of management and business skills. There are approximately 16 schools worldwide, located mainly in Canada and the United Kingdom, mostly as part of a Foundation/Associate's level or equivalent. These programmes ranges from a clear division between spa therapy, massage, aesthetics and spa, salon, resort management courses, to a primarily spa therapy, massage, aesthetics programmes that include short business and management modules, significant development given the huge amount of managers/spa directors starting from positions at the therapist level and heading to managerial jobs, providing them with some basic-level management as essential baseline knowledge for their potential future. A continuing education and on-the-job training is an essential component for them as they move into management positions (GSWS, 2012).

In addition we can divide further spa related qualification in:

- Vocational education, career preparation with focus on specific competencies teaching, practically assessed and recognised by specific certificate or diploma award (Cohen & Bodeker, 2008);
- Higher education, degree-level education aiming to broad understanding of a field with critical thinking and lifelong learning skills awarded by both undergraduate degrees as well as postgraduate qualifications including Graduate Certificates, Graduate Diplomas, Masters Degrees as well as PhDs and professional doctorates. Providers are generally universities or private colleges (Cohen & Bodeker, 2008);
- In-house education, provided by a company to its employees focused on specific tasks, practical skills and services standards requirements, constitutes majority of post-entry education. May or may not lead to formal qualifications. Many spa and product companies developed own training programs for

© 2018 OAXIES® LTD

operations and treatments (Cohen & Bodeker, 2008);

- Workplace training, students placement to obtain practical business and/or therapy experiences, developing specific skills. Can be paid or unpaid, organised between employer and educational service provider for vocational training or higher education diploma (Cohen & Bodeker, 2008).

It is important to remember that the regulatory environment for the spa industry varies widely and varies from minimum or no legislative requirements in some countries to various models of industrial self-regulation and government regulation, that can act to protect specific job titles or practice scope as well as regulating educational requirements and the right to practice. To solve this problem, specific companies have tried to differentiate themselves by setting their own standards. All over the world there are many associations and accreditation bodies with different standards of education, assessment and licensing, which lead to vast variations in the standards of therapists, service employees and managers and there is a need to standardise these qualifications (Cohen & Bodeker, 2008).

Furthermore, the education linked to the spa is wide and available through formal and informal channels, which vary according to the global position, both by public and private bodies that offer both vocational education and higher education as well as "in-house" provided by spas and product companies (Cohen & Bodeker, 2008).

In United Kingdom:

- ITEC, The International Therapy Examination Council (ITEC) offering beauty, business, complementary therapy and sports-related qualifications worldwide, providing nationally and internationally recognised qualifications (ITEC, 2018; Cohen & Bodeker, 2008);
- CIBTAC, Confederation of International Beauty Therapy and Cosmetology, providing education and training to beauty and holistic therapists worldwide offering CIBTAC Awards,

recognised internationally, by accrediting schools (CIBTAC, 2018; Cohen & Bodeker, 2008);

- CIDESCO, Comité International Esthetique et de Cosmétologie, world's major international beauty therapy association founded in 1946 with approved schools around the world (CIDESCO, 2018; Cohen & Bodeker, 2008);
- HABIA, Hairdressing and Beauty Industry Association, UK government's approved standard setting body for hair, beauty, nails and spa therapy. It creates the standards for all qualifications including UK National Vocational Qualifications (NVQs), Scottish Vocational Qualifications (SVQs), Apprenticeships, Diplomas and Foundation degrees, as well as industry codes of practice (HABIA, 2018; Cohen & Bodeker, 2008);
- City and Guilds, leading vocational awarding body in the UK, with short awards for recognition of prior learning (RPL) (City & Guilds, 2018; Cohen and Bodeker, 2008);
- VTCT, Vocational Training Charitable Trust, government approved Awarding Body offering NVQs, SVQs and other vocationally related qualifications (VRQs) in beauty therapy, hairdressing, holistic and complementary therapies and sports and fitness (VTCT, 2018; Cohen & Bodecker).

In the USA:

- NCBTMB, National Certification Board for Therapeutic Massage & Bodywork, establish a certification program and uphold a national standard of excellence in therapeutic massage and bodywork (NCBTMB, 2018; Cohen & Bodeker, 2008);
- COMTA, Commission On Massage Therapy Accreditation, non-profit independent body, accrediting schools and programmes that provide post-secondary certificates, diplomas or degrees in the practice of massage therapy and bodywork (COMTA, 2018; Cohen & Bodeker, 2008);
- FSMBT, Federation of State Massage Therapy Boards, non-profit organisation that launched a new Massage & Bodywork Licensing Examination, MBLEx, supporting Massage Therapy Boards across the US (FSMBT, 2018; Cohen &

© 2018 OAXIES® LTD

Bodeker, 2008).

In Australia:

- AQF, Australian Qualifications Framework, nationally recognised accreditation framework that links together all qualifications issued by secondary schools, vocational education and training (VET) providers and higher education institutions also allowing individual educational institutions to develop own qualifications (AQF, 2018; Cohen & Bodeker, 2008);
- CSHISC, Service Skills Australia and Community Services and Health Industry Skills Council, national Industry Skills Council for tourism, hospitality, hairdressing and beauty, fitness and recreation specifying training packages, spa education in the Australian vocational training sector, accredited spa education in the higher education (Cohen & Bodeker, 2008).

In South Africa:

- AHPCSA, Allied Health Professions Council of South Africa, statutory health body to control all allied health professions (AHPCSA, 2018; Cohen & Bodeker, 2008);
- MTA, Massage Therapy Association–South Africa, the only professional association representing the interests of Therapeutic Massage Therapists in South Africa (MTA, 2018; Cohen & Bodeker, 2008).

2.3 THE ITALIAN SPA INDUSTRY

The wellness sector in Italy is made up of several independent but at the same time complementary segments, with a high degree of specialisation involving about 31,000 companies and 56,000 workers (ISTAT, 2008). Italy has always been a leading country in the sector having a strong tradition in thermal spa, with 171 localities and 370 spas (Becheri & Quirino, 2011; Ferrari, 2014).

Unfortunately, currently more than 80% of Italian spas are not managed by a manager, which is one of the reasons why, despite the steady growth of the sector, numerous spa areas are not profitable or closed (Minardi, 2017).

A specialised manager, able to manage every aspect, is the key to the proper functioning, especially economic, of a spa. The role of spa manager is of strategic, commercial and financial management and must therefore be covered by a figure who, through training and tendency of character, is able to develop and manage all these delicate variables (Minardi, 2017). In fact, the management of the various areas of the spa, with organisational and managerial commitments, are intended for managerial figures. Spa managers and spa directors in order to conduct the activities correctly, must be profoundly aware of all the technical, managerial, legal and financial aspects (Bovero & Virgintino, 2013). The execution of practical tasks such as treatments or other services should not be part of the role but unfortunately, in Italy, this division does not exist and spa managers face almost all aspects of the structure, including treatments in the cabin, often being a technical figure, beautician, operator, with a three-year or four-year training course, to then become a manager or technical director of the spa without an adequate education (Bovero & Virgintino, 2013).

However, some structural categories need to be taken into consideration, analysing specific divisions, in order to interpret well the Italian system of spas and wellness centres. First of all, the distinction between spas and wellness centres, starting from the early eighties, when the first spas and beauty salon began to spread.

The primary resource of thermal spas was founded on the offer of natural thermal waters from therapeutic and prevention properties. For this reason, we talk about spa treatments and therefore of thermal establishments or structures within which thermal services are provided, with recognised therapeutic efficacy by the National Health Service. On the other hand, the goal of the wellness centres is to make guests feel comfortable under the physical and psychological aspects, focusing the activity on the aesthetic aspects, on the improvement of the body and the

© 2018 OAXIES® LTD

image. They were born autonomously and almost in opposition, as an innovative offer (Becheri & Quirino, 2012).

Although in all of Europe, the spa destinations changed therapeutic position towards a more diversified range of wellness, in order to address new market segments, satisfying new types of tourists, and overcome the crisis, Italian spa companies started only in the last two decades of the twentieth century. This is mainly due to not losing public funding as the spa offer was promoted through family practitioners and word of mouth (Becheri & Quirino, 2011; Ferrari, 2014). Towards the 90s, then, when the relationship between the two markets changed, thermal spas started to reposition themselves towards wellness sector, not only offering health treatments aimed particularly at the elderly, but combining well-being chains alongside their own structures, creating, in fact, the new segment of "thermal wellness". In this way, they entered in direct competition with wellness centres, expanding their role as resting places for mental and physical regeneration (Becheri & Quirino, 2011; Ferrari 2014).

The aim was to create an integrated offer, combining spa treatments with fitness, relaxation and beauty services (AICEB, 2010) transforming spas into wellness centres (Ferrari, 2014).

The reduction of funds allocated by the State for the purchase of spa services, still paid by the National Health Service, has led this transformation of the spa offer and the consequent need to increase the flow of private customers. Furthermore, the Italian Law Reordering the Thermal Spa Sector (Law no. 323/2000) was introduced, stating that the word "spa" can only refer to thermal companies, thus trying to reduce the widespread confusion on the terminology (Ferrari, 2014). Spas are therefore gradually and increasingly becoming independent and part of the tourism sector at the same time (Faroldi et al., 2007). Indeed, the 85 percent of the thermal baths nowadays have a space dedicated to wellness (Becheri & Quirino, 2012), operating sometimes independently and, in other cases, together with the thermal structure.

Traditional Beauty Therapist Path

Vocational Qualification Certificate in Beauty Therapy | 2 years | EQF 3
→ Licence to Practice in Beauty Therapy | 1 year

Beauty Therapist Path to Fulfill Compulsory Schooling

Qualification of Professional Education in Beauty Cure Operator | 3 years | EQF 3
→ Professional Education Diploma in Beauty Treatments Technician | 1 year | EQF 4
→ Superior Technician Diploma in Spa Management | 2 years | EQF 5
→ UNIVERSITY 3-8 years | EQF 6, 7, 8

Mineral Spring Spa Director Path

Bachelor Degree (e.g. Economics, Communication Studies) | 3 years | EQF 6
→ Master Degree (e.g. Marketing, Management) | 2 years | EQF 7
→ 2nd Level Master Degree in Health Management | 1 year | EQF 8
→ + 5 years management experience (Health industry) or + 7 years management experience (Non-Health Industry)

CIDESCO International Diploma Path

CIDESCO Diploma Spa & Beauty Manager Management & Quality Standards | 120 hours | Not EQF Accredited
→ CIDESCO Diploma Spa & Beauty Manager Marketing & Communication | 120 hours | Not EQF Accredited
→ CIDESCO Diploma Spa & Beauty Manager Business, Events & Rituals | 120 hours | Not EQF Accredited
→ CIDESCO Diploma Spa & Beauty Manager International Diploma | 80 hours | Not EQF Accredited

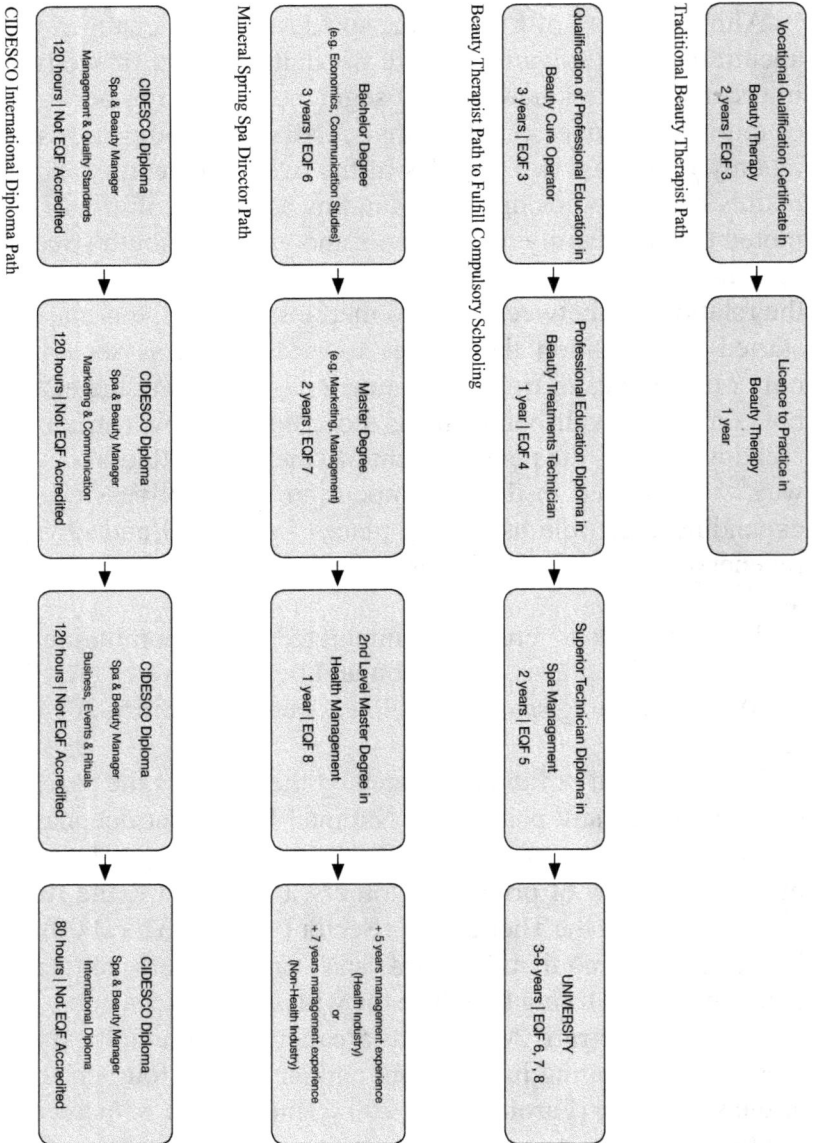

Fig. 1: Italian Educational and Training Paths

© 2018 OAXIES® LTD

In Italy, spas, wellness centres and beauty centres are regulated by Law n. 1 of 4 January 1990. The requisite for obtaining the authorisation to open an activity in the wellness sector is the possession of the vocational beautician qualification gained according to the training provided for by the aforementioned law. The owner must be in possession, or hire somebody in charge with the qualification of beautician, who has the requisites required by law and who can play the role of technical director (Virgintino & Bovero, 2013; Law n. 1 of 4 January 1990).

In the majority of the Italian regions, for those who are still underage or still have to fulfil compulsory education and training (those aged between 14 and 18) the professional qualification of Beautician is reached with a path called "Istruzione e Formazione Professionale" (IeFP), which provides for a three-year path composed of: a first common year both for the hairdresser and for the beautician; a second year of in-depth study for the chosen address; and a third year, including a period of internship, professionalizing, with the passing of the examination to obtain the Vocational Qualification of Education and Professional Training of Beautician (3rd level EQF). With this title it is possible to enrol in the annual courses of "Vocational Diploma of Education and Professional Training of Aesthetic Treatments Technician" , a 4th year post-qualification, for the acquisition of the License to Practice of Beautician, or to continue the studies at secondary schools, to obtain the high school leaving diploma/baccalaureate, or at "Istituti Tecnici Superiori" (ITS), which are 2-year Post Diploma Technical Specialisation courses, referring to the areas considered as priorities for the economic development and competitiveness of the country, equivalent to a Foundation degree (Enaip Veneto, 2018; Opera Armida Barelli, 2018; Istituti Tecnici Superiori, 2018).

However, being a regional qualification, in some regions the route can vary, as regions may have different regulations (Ecipar, 2018; Regione Emilia Romagna, 2018).

For those who have instead fulfilled compulsory education

and training and are adults there is a different path which provides:

Professional training courses are planned by the Regions with the most representative regional associations at national level. The course is triennial with compulsory attendance: 2 years of qualification and one of specialisation to obtain the License to Practice. At the end of the three-year period a special qualification exam is required, which takes place at the training centres of the trade associations in the presence of a regional inspector. Precisely, the law provides that the Vocational Professional Qualification of Beautician (EQF Level 3) can be achieved after a two-year regional qualification course, with a minimum of 900 hours per year, 1800 hours in total, alternatively followed by:

- License to Practice qualifying specialisation course lasting a year of 600 hours;
- Or 1 year working experience in a beautician company;
- Or apprenticeship plus 1 year of full-time qualified work, followed by the regional course of 300 hours of theoretical qualification, integrating the acquired practical knowledge to gain the License to Practice;
- Or have spent a period of no less than three years of qualified work as an employee, full-time, in a beautician, and followed by the regional course of 300 hours (Ecipar, 2018; The Law for All, 2018; Regione Emilia Romagna, 2018).

After this course of study, it is possible become a technical director in a beauty and wellness centre but there is no defined path to become a spa manager. There are some associations and private companies that offer short courses providing a certificate in spa management such as CIDESCO Italia. Moreover some universities and Post Diploma Technical Specialisation courses (ITS) with Hospitality or Management programmes have started to include 1 or more modules related to spa management at respectively EQF Level 7 and 5 (CIDESCO, 2018; ITS, 2018; Luiss Business School, 2018). Also, the Opera Armida Barelli of Trento offers the new Advanced Professional Training Path "Superior Technician for the Management of the Wellness Center"

© 2018 OAXIES® LTD

(Rossi, 2015).

In addition, the requirement in order to become spa director of a Mineral Spring Spa (ISPA, 2018), owned and managed by the State, according to Legislative Decree n. 171 of 4th August 2016, is to be included into a national list, as they are still bodies of the National Health Service. To be part of that it is necessary to be in possession of: master degree; proven management experience of at least five years in the health sector or seven years in other sectors, managerial autonomy and direct responsibility for human, technical and financial resources, and most importantly, the obtainment of a certificate issued at the end of the training course in the fields of health economic and management. The aforementioned courses are organised and activated by the regions and in collaboration with universities or other accredited public or private subjects operating in the field of management training (Ministero della Salute, 2018).

2.4 CONCLUSION

In conclusion, as emerged from the literature, there are different spa associations and accrediting bodies worldwide with diverse standards of education, assessment and licensing with the need to standardise these qualifications (Cohen & Bodeker, 2008).

Furthermore, there are some shortcomings in education for spa management roles, which mean that there is a lack of skills in the field. The need for advanced qualifications, including postgraduate qualifications, is given by the demand for higher levels of education. Educational service providers must therefore focus more on spa management and customer service, in particular on business management and training of personal and team leadership, and finally on the development of specific standards and qualifications for the harmonisation of standards (Cohen & Bodeker, 2008). It is therefore important to analyse the phenomenon in order to provide suggestions and identify the steps to be taken to overcome them.

3 RESEARCH METHODOLOGY

3.1 RESEARCH PHILOSOPHY, APPROACH AND ORIENTATION

The selection of the appropriate methodology for research is important in order to have the bases and methods to achieve the purpose, goals and objectives of the research (Bryman, 2015; Saunders et al., 2009). The philosophical paradigms are those who guide these methodologies that include an ontology (the nature of reality), an epistemology (the consideration on an acceptable knowledge) and an axiology (the personal values of the researcher in the study) (Bryman, 2015; Creswell, 2013; Saunders et al., 2009).

The methodology chosen for this study is an interpretative paradigm that follows the ontological assumptions of subjectivism, for which reality or truth is determined by the interpretation in different contexts, social phenomena are socially and inter-subjectively structured realities. It is therefore fundamental the scholar's active engagement with the research participants, for the purpose of a truthful image of the social dynamics influencing the research question (Crotty, 1998; Saunders et al., 2009; Creswell, 2013; Silverman, 2016).

The adoption of the interpretative paradigm normally predisposes the use of an inductive approach because of its link with the exploratory studies for the construction of a theory with a question based on the observation of the phenomenon, which allows the researcher to explore the perceptions of the participants (Bryman, 2015; Gray, 2014; Creswell, 2013; Veal, 2011;

Saunders, et al., 2009).

The interpretative paradigm is also linked to qualitative strategies, which are based on the assumption that social reality is a subjective experience, continuously constructed and linked to the social context. The aims are the description, understanding and meaning with the use of small cases, to give an in-depth knowledge of the social phenomenon to be linked and analysed directly to the world and to the opinions of the participants (Denzin & Lincoln, 2013; Veal, 2011; Corbin & Strauss, 2008; Gratton & Jones, 2004).

3.2 RESEARCH DESIGN

Data collection and analysis is guided by the research design framework that for this study is qualitatively oriented in the form of a comparative case study design (Yin, 2009). Case studies are flexible qualitative methods that can lead to a thorough and complete investigation, studying complex social phenomena at various levels of analysis, in their contexts of uniqueness, completeness and real life (Denzin & Lincoln, 2013; Thomas, 2011; Yin, 2009).

The authors have deployed 19 semi-structured interviews and questionnaires to Italian or working in Italy spa managers (11), spa directors (2), industry leaders such as association presidents (2), consultants (2), trainers (1) and representative of trade associations (1). Each interviewed was selected following certain criteria like the type of role, position and experience in the industry, knowledge of the topic.

3.3 RESEARCH METHODS

The author conducted 19 semi-structured interviews and questionnaires, for their depth and ability to adapt the tone to different interlocutors and contexts, so as to give the possibility to the researcher to move forward on the topic explored, and give further opportunities for clarification by tackling the problems (Silverman, 2016; Saunders, 2009). Interviews and questionnaires have

© 2018 OAXIES® LTD

been conducted via e-mail, Skype or by telephone and recorded with a dictaphone, to help focusing on answers (Veal & Burton, 2014; Veal, 2011; Crang & Cook, 2007).

3.4 SAMPLING TECHNIQUES & LINE OF ENQUIRY

The collection of rich and deep data in the qualitative research starts with a small sample of participants and acquiring a privileged vision. For this reason, the chosen sampling strategy procedure is purposive (Bryman, 2015; Veal & Burton, 2014; Veal, 2011; Saunders et al., 2009). Indeed, 19 semi-structured interviews and questionnaires have been developed to Italian or working in Italy spa managers and directors, industry leaders such as consultants, trainers, training association presidents and representative of trade associations, giving them the chance to explain their opinions on the importance of basic qualifications and experiences, the pros and cons of the current educational system and the management skills for the Italian spa industry.

In doing so the line of enquiry followed was:

- Career pathway;
- Education & training pathway;
- Basic required and expected skills for spa manager role;
- Expected skills recruiting a member owning International Spa Management Degree or Spa Management short course or Beautician Vocational Qualification;
- Required and expected experience;
- Required and expected education & training;
- Barriers in the Italian educational & training system;
- Knowledge, benchmarking and effectiveness of educational & training Italian and International systems.

3.5 ETHICS

Through ethics the researcher will have a particular conduct following a behaviour in respect of the rights in the research in order to prevent a participant from suffering psychological, financial or social damage and there are various ethical considerations to be put in place, identifying any damage and ensuring the presence of mechanisms able to remove them (Silverman, 2016; Gray, 2014; Denzin & Lincoln, 2013;Saunders et al., 2009).

In the following table the ethical considerations adopted:

A	**Consent** Participants informed about the purpose and use of the research. Children not recruited;
B	**Deception** Not used within the study;
C	**Debriefing** Participants debriefed verbally;
D	**Withdrawal from the investigation** Participants are free to withdrawn from the study at anytime. Participants will be aware cannot withdrawn from investigation once primary data analysed and disseminated;
E	**Confidentiality** Data generated not to be passed onto third parties, stored safely and used only for this study. Consent forms and data stored separately and securely. Collection of data relevant to the study being undertaken. Protect of participant's anonymity unless they have given their permission to be identified (stated on the Informed Consent Form). Data will be returned to participants or destroyed if consent is not given after the fact, or if a participant withdraws;
F	**Protection of participants** No risk of physical, psychological or emotional harm greater than encountered ordinary life;
G	**Observation research** Not related.
H	**Giving advice** Student is not putting himself in a position of authority from which to provide advice and will refer participants to suitably qualified and appropriate professionals;
I	**Research undertaken in public places** Observation of the laws of obscenity and public decency, religious and cultural sensitivities;

© 2018 OAXIES® LTD

J	**Data protection** Compliance with the Data Protection Act and the University's Good Scientific Practice;
K	**Animal Rights** Not related;
L	**Environmental protection** Not related.

Tab. 1: Ethics Considerations

3.6 VERIFICATION CRITERIA

Reliability, authenticity, robustness and rigor are the principles that define the admissibility and quality of the research key findings. Specifically, rigor refers to attention to detail, ensured by the debriefing method to correctly present the information obtained; while the robustness to the ability of the methodology to remain steadfast in difficult situations ensured in this case by the collection of data with semi-structured interviews and questionnaires in line with ethical considerations (Gray, 2014; Veal, 2011).

In the table below the measures taken to address threats characterising the chosen methodology (Crang & Cook, 2007; Corbin & Strauss, 2008; Creswell, 2013; Gray, 2014).

Issues	Actions
• Bias • Value-led • Internal invalidity	Use of electronic devices while ecording the interview; Self-reflective approach.

Tab. 2: Verification Criteria

3.7 DATA ANALYSIS PROCEDURES

The analysis of data through the interpretative paradigm must take into account the dependence of data on human cognition; and for this we must have the ability to go beyond the dualism of this role (Bryman, 2015; Denzin & Lincoln; 2013; Saunders et al., 2009). For this reason the analysis of the discourse was adopted to elaborate the themes that emerged (Potter, 2012; 1996). The answers were then codified and interpreted, linked to themes and categories through the inductive approach, to understand the judgments, perceptions and experiences of the interviewees (Minichiello et al., 1990).

© 2018 OAXIES® LTD

4 ANALYSIS AND DISCUSSION

4.1 INTRODUCTION

In this chapter the author deploys a discourse analysis of all interviews 19 interviews to spa managers, spa directors, industry leaders such as trainers, consultants, training association and trade associations representatives, working within the Italian spa industry.

Each interviewed was selected following certain criteria like the type of role, position and experience in the industry, knowledge of the topic.

4.2 DISCOURSE ANALYSIS

The interviews and questionnaires have been treated individually, divided according to the belonging professional category, and using the analytical framework and key lines emerging from the literature, the key findings have been recombined. The themes identified as common has been discussed, as well as a reflection on those that are specific to each category. Interviews and questionnaires have been conducted with spa managers & directors (14), spa consultants (2) trainers (1) and industry leaders such as trade associations representatives & training association presidents (3).

Interestingly the themes emerged are common between all the 4 professional categories. These have been divided and put in a table for a better understanding.

4.3 DATA ANALYSIS

The analysis highlighted that the career for the most totality of interviewed has been in hospitality or in the beauty industry and for a minority in the fitness & wellness industry. While the training undertaken has been mainly in beauty and complimentary therapy or academic degree plus some specialisation courses.

In the table below are illustrated the key findings:

Experience more important;
Beautician Vocational Qualification and Academic Degree useful but not necessary;
Barriers Italian spa management education and training development: obsolescence of Italian regulations and laws, labor costs, high salary;
Unsatisfactory Italian spa management educational and training system;
Improvement suggested for Italian spa management educational and training system: internship & recognition of the spa manager figure;
Willingness from representatives of trade associations and training associations to improve spa management educational and training system, adapting the regulations.

Tab. 3: Key Findings

4.3.1 SKILLS

The most important skills required for a spa manager role that have been identified are in human resources, marketing, finance, revenue management, IT and communication skills. While wellness, beauty and spa knowledge, technical skills, operations management, management skills and leadership are recognised less important.

HR	9
Marketing	8
Finance	7
Revenue	6
Communications Skills	6
IT	5
Wellness Knowledge	4
Operations Management	4
Management Skills	4

© 2018 OAXIES® LTD

Beauty Knowledge	4
Technical Skills	3
Spa Knowledge	3
Leadership	3

Tab. 4: Required Basic Skills for Spa Manager Role

Interestingly, leadership is the top one skill for the expected skills when hiring a spa manager, as well as operations management. The knowledge of languages is also considered important on the same level with human resources, finance and creativity and resourcefulness that have not been mention for required skills. Communication skills, problem solving, marketing and management are deemed less important.

Leadership	7
Operations Management	5
Languages Knowledge	5
HR	5
Creativity	6
Resourcefulness	5
Finance	4
Communication Skills	4
Problem Solving	4
Marketing	4
Management Skills	3

Tab. 5: Expected Basic Skills for Spa Manager Role

It is interesting to note that the most important and ideal expected education and training when hiring a spa manager is the high school leaving diploma, then a massage or beauty therapy qualification, languages knowledge, marketing and management qualifications.

High School Leaving Diploma	4
Massage Qualification	3
Languages	3
Beauty Therapy Qualification	3
Management	3

Marketing	3

Tab. 6: Expected Spa Manager Education & Training

Leadership is again the top skills when hiring a member of the staff with a spa management academic degree, to then move to languages knowledge. Then problem solving, management skills, international industry knowledge, creativity and communication skills, all on the same level.

Leadership	6
Languages Knowledge	4
Problem Solving	3
Marketing	3
Management Skills	3
International Industry Knowledge	3
Creativity	3
Communication Skills	3

Tab. 7: Expected Skills Member of Staff with Spa Management Academic Degree

Only finance and human resources are the skills identified as important for a member of the staff who attended a spa management short course.

Finance	4
HR	3

Tab. 8: Expected Skills Staff Member with Spa Management Short Course

Finally, the skills for a staff member owing a Beautician Vocational Qualification are more related to the knowledge of treatments, beauty and cosmetic. Indeed, the treatment knowledge is the most important skills, followed by revenue management and empathy to relate with customers. This indicate a competence at operational level in a beauty salon and not the management for a spa.

Spa Manager at Hotel Bellevue Suites & Spa: "As I see it, they are not able to manage a spa but a beauty salon instead."

© 2018 OAXIES® LTD

Treatment Knowledge	6
Revenue	5
Empathy	5
Cleaning	4
Cosmetic Knowledge	3
Beauty Knowledge	3

Tab. 9: Expected Skills Staff Member with Beautician Vocational Qualification

4.3.2 EXPERIENCE & EDUCATION

It is interesting that, when asked what type of education and training expected when recruiting a spa manager, some of them state that experience is more important than education and training

Director of Spa & Soft Medical Operations at Terme di Saturnia: "If referred to the Italian market which, at the moment, does not offer, with just few exceptions, structured paths, we prefer people from the tourism sector (wellness and hospitality), marketing and linguistic, as well as aesthetic or cosmetic."

and

Spa Manager at Gritti Palace Hotel: "More than education I would expect experience in the field."

and

Trainer & General Manager at Comfort Zone: "Besides the didactic and scholastic path, I look at the experience in tourist and accommodation facilities."

and

Ceo & Founder at bbspa&partners: "I am interested more in the professional path than education and training."

This argument was confirmed and clarified when it was explicitly asked if the years of experience were a more important skill than the years of education/qualification or both important.

Spa Manager at Mirtillo Rosso Family Hotel: "The experience is definitely more important, but the qualification helps to live a more edifying experience."

and

Spa Manager at Gritti Palace Hotel: "They are both important but on the scale the experience weighs more especially if in international contexts."

and

Spa Manager at H10 Hotels Roma: "They are both important, but the years of experience are those that form and make you grow, education is the basis on which to work."

and

Spa Manager at Hotel Terme Venezia Abano Terme: "Yes !!! I think it is then the experience in the field, the work, to select the staff itself, to give us and tell us which are the more or less suitable people. It is not in the books that come out the soft skills of each of us!"

Or suggesting a gap in the Italian educational system in this regard

Director of Spa & Soft Medical Operations at Terme di Saturnia: "There is no alternative in reference to the Italian market today, in general terms the difference is always made by the quality of the people and not their history."

However, once asked how many years of experience were necessary before covering a spa manager role it has been difficult to determine the minimum years required.

© 2018 OAXIES® LTD

A Beautician Professional Qualification for a spa manager role has been considered desirable but not necessary, in particular for the knowledge of treatments to be offered. Likewise, a Bachelor Degree for a spa manager role was deemed desirable but not necessary. In particular, they were considered a plus academic degrees in Business & Economic Management, Marketing Management, Tourism & Hospitality Management, Service Management. In particular, the educational and training path suggested for a spa manager role has been an academic degree plus a specialisation course.

Director of Spa & Soft Medical Operations at Terme di Saturnia: "If present, Higher Education or University paths oriented to the Spa Industry, or alternatively hospitality."

and

Spa Manager at Hotel Bel Soggiorno Beauty Spa: "A path that can take advantage of both technical and work-related know-how in the field of wellness, but above all a managerial training ..."

and

Spa Director at Hotel Milano Alpen Spa: "In Great Britain and the US there are good universities with interesting degree courses, in Italy we are at the beginning for universities, with the exception of universities in physical education and Sports."

and

Spa Manager at Dolce Vita Hotel Preidlhof: "High School Leaving Diploma and academic degree, an advantage would be the combination of a beauty therapy school to be able to assess the quality and know the techniques."

and

Wellness Consultant Self-employed at CJ Advisor Wellness & Sport: "Therapist Training and an Academic Spa Management Course of minimum 1 year"

and

Spa Manager at H10 Hotels Roma: "Economic Bachelor Degree or Spa Management and practical training in a Spa."

and

Spa Manager at Hotel Terme Venezia Abano Terme: "At the moment Business Economic, in the absence of a more specific path."

and

Chairman of CIDESCO Italia: "Possibly a degree course, then specialised training courses and a lot of workplace training."

and

President of AISA: "Specific degree and training in Germany, the Netherlands, and the United States."

and

Head of the professional qualification area for beauty and hairdressing at ECIPAR Bologna: "Undertake a complete training course: qualification as a beautician plus a specialisation and then a training course that provides skills in management, administration, marketing and personnel management."

Also, a continuous update and study was the most common advice to give to those starting out in the spa industry.

Spa Manager at Hotel Bel Soggiorno Beauty Spa: "Always update and remain active and enterprising."

© 2018 OAXIES® LTD

and

Spa Director at Hotel Milano Alpen SPA: "Studying, studying, working with determination, getting to know the competitors."

and

Spa Manager at H10 Hotels Roma: "To always update, it is a world in constant evolution."

and

Spa Manager at Dolce Vita Hotel Preidlhof: "Undertake various internship during the studies to see, understand and try everything…".

4.3.3 BARRIERS IN THE ITALIAN EDUCATIONAL AND TRAINING SYSTEM

When asked if the role of ideologies in Italy is determining the managerial opportunities, in particular the difference between Wellness and Health Well-being, most of them were unable to answer, as unaware of certain Italian laws, while others have referred to the field of prevention and welfare and the clear necessity of its evolvement for the development of spa manager figure.

Director of Spa & Soft Medical Operations at Terme di Saturnia: "The Wellness sector in Italy has an ancestor called Terme, a sector that, after the golden years of welfarism, has in turn proved incapable of generating a leading level of management. The demonstration is that almost all the most important figures in the industry do not come from the sector itself."

Or underlining the great opportunities the wellness concept development can offer

Spa Manager at Hotel Bellevue Suites & SPA: "There is no doubt, wellness is part of the health sector, positioned in the seg-

ment called prevention. Which role it has or it will have in the future depends on the entrepreneurs, the type of managers they hire, and the Spa Manager skills related to the concept of wellness. Wellness has enormous power, it depends on us Spa Manager if we can exploit it".

Or suggesting the union and cooperation between the two sectors

Chairman of CIDESCO Italia: "The concept of wellness, in its broadest sense, is influencing all sectors in detail and represents today an incredible opportunity at the business level."

and

President of AISA: "The industry starts to link the two factors."

and

Spa Manager at Hotel Terme Venezia Abano Terme: "I believe it is right that there are differences between those involved in wellness and those in medicine and health, but I also think that close collaboration is necessary in certain settings.".

Some of interviewed, despite working within the industry, were not aware of certain Italian regulations and laws, in particular Italian Law Reordering the Thermal Spa Sector Law no. 323/2000 and Discipline of the Beautician Activity Law no. 1/1990, and to the question whether these laws and trade associations were strengthening cultural and ideological barriers by acting in the same way as barriers to the development of the educational and training system, they could not answer. Others instead recognised the obsolescence of Italian regulations and laws as barriers for the development of education and training.

Spa Manager at Therasia Resort Sea & Spa: "Absolutely yes, this law is made to create fictitious professions linked to purely

© 2018 OAXIES® LTD

*regional courses and excluding figures with decades of experi-
ence in the spa."*

It is interesting to note that the representatives of trade associations and training association are aware of the need to change
and expand the law in order to make changes to the Italian training system for spa managers.

*Chairman of CIDESCO Italia: "...The law 1/90 is obsolete
and the trade associations do not implement effective strategies."*

and

*President of AISA: "In Italy, the bureaucracy and lobbies
keep their interests tight, this slows down the processes of educational growth."*

and

*Head of the professional qualification area for beauty and
hairdressing at Ecipar Bologna: "The law 1/90 is undoubtedly
to be reviewed. The industry associations (my knowledge is addressed to CNA) are actually working to update the legislation in
order to adapt it to the current needs of the sector."*

Or highlighting the gap and backwardness in the Italian educational system

*Director of Spa & Soft Medical Operations at Terme di Satur-
nia: "About this theme there is an absolute void."*

and

*Spa Manager at Relais del Nuovo Benessere Solofra Palace
Hotel & Resort: "In Italy, at the moment, the three-year beautician vocation qualification diploma is the only requirement to
open a wellness activity and this still involves staff who are not
always qualified or in any case ready to manage the complex*

world of spas.".

4.3.4 KNOWLEDGE, BENCHMARKING AND EFFECTIVENESS OF EDUCATIONAL AND TRAINING SYSTEMS

Most respondents are unaware of the education and training system in other countries; also representatives of training and trade associations, only a minority.

Trainer & General Manager Comfort Zone: "If we exclude England and Holland, little else. In Italy it is starting thanks to sporadic initiatives managed by private individuals (eg. Institute Opera Armida Barelli in Rovereto, Trento)."

and

Wellness Consultant Self-employed at CJ Advisor Wellness & Sport: "UK, Switzerland, Germany, USA, Australia, Canada.".

Moreover, the interviewed could not recognise a benchmarking or competitiveness of Italian spa management educational system against the training and educational system in other countries but only dissatisfaction and backwardness.

Spa Director at Hotel Milano Alpen Spa: "Unfortunately, the Italian university education system in this sector is at the beginning of a path that sees other nations, in particular the United States, at the forefront of the quality of courses and studies in the sector."

and

Spa Manager at Hotel Bellevue Suites & Spa : "The wellness sector in Italy is not well defined, so neither is training but I can not give an evaluation because I do not know the situations in other countries in depth."

 © 2018 OAXIES® LTD

and

Trainer & General Manager Comfort Zone: "Currently lower than expected."

and

Spa manager at Hotel Terme Venezia Abano Terme: "There is not.".

And the willingness to improve it

President of AISA: "Several years behind the times, but as an association we are working on it."

Despite the majority were unaware of training and educational system in other countries the benchmarking and competitiveness of these have been described as more structured for the spa manager figure.

Spa Director at Hotel Milano Alpen Spa : "In Italy we have a very good professional preparation as regards secondary schools of beauty and massage therapy but we lack at university level in the strictly managerial aspect of the spa. In other nations, excluding Germany, it seems to me that the level of vocational schools is a little lower, while the university level on spa management is better."

and

Chairman of CIDESCO Italia: "Probably a better structuring of the 'Spa Business System', which in the past years has developed faster than Italy."

The current status of Italian training and educational systems for spa manager has been described unsatisfactory, superficial, defective and incomplete.

Spa Manager at Mirtillo Rosso Family Hotel: "Too free! And for some courses too superficial."

and

Spa Manager at Gritti Palace Hotel: "I believe that in Italy the courses of spa managers are nothing more than seminars that give general information but do not give an effective training, especially from an administrative and commercial point of view. This is reflected every time I compare myself with some person who has attended these courses."

and

Wellness Consultant Self-employed at CJ Advisor Wellness & Sport: "I believe that there is a lack of academic education in spa/wellness management."

and

Spa Manager at Hotel Terme Venezia Abano Terme: "Virtually nil."

and
Ceo & Founder at bbspa&partners: "Zero."

and

Spa Manager at Relais del Nuovo Benessere Solofra Palace Hotel & Resort: "Incomplete"

and

Spa Manager at Ringo Hotel Baja Sardinia: "Still rather lacking".

Or pointing out the lack of recognition of the role

© 2018 OAXIES® LTD

Spa Manager at Hotel Bel Soggiorno Beauty Spa: "*I do not find the system yet ready to technically prepare the figure of the spa manager, unfortunately as many 'new' professions it not yet has a place in the world of education.*"

Or, appreciating the attempt by some training institutions, it has been considered growing

Spa Manager at H10 Hotels Roma: "*It is a growing education, until few years ago it was the beauty therapist who was covering the role of manager, but now it has been understood that there is a need for trained figures.*"

and

Spa Director at Hotel Milano Alpen Spa: "*Deficit, but growing.*"

and

Spa Manager at Therasia Resort Sea & Spa: "*Good, the only one is the CIDESCO course in Spa Management.*"

and

Chairman of CIDESCO Italia: "*It is growing rapidly. In 2018 the CIDESCO International Diploma in Beauty & Spa Management was also activated in Italy and this is a very important step for the development of the sector in our country.*"

and

Director of Spa & Soft Medical Operations at Terme di Saturnia: "*There is only one path really oriented towards this goal: Higher Education in Superior Technician in the Management of Wellness Centres at Opera Armida Barelli of Rovereto (Biennium).*"

Once again, regarding the competitiveness of the Italian Spa industry in relation to recruiting effective, competent and talented spa managers, the majority of respondents have instead pointed out what the problems were, according to their experience.

Addressing the problems to the development of the sector

Director of Spa & Soft Medical Operations at Terme di Saturnia: "The key word is talent, which we still lack to recognise. On the other fronts the market is growing."

or

Spa Director at Hotel Milano Alpen Spa: "We have a spa / wellness sector which, in terms of quality, variety and quantity, has no equal in the world but needs to be updated and relaunched."

Or on the one hand, the problem is addressed to those not hiring young people

Spa Manager at Hotel Bel Soggiorno Beauty Spa: "I believe that Italian professionals often live up to foreigners, the only difference is that the industry is not yet ready to invest in young people which is a lack of mentality."

While on the other hand, to those hiring young people without experience

Spa Manager at Gritti Palace Hotel: "At this moment I do not believe it is competitive at all. In many luxury spas the role of spa manager is covered by girls who are too young and with little experience, obviously because of costs, but they are not able to develop a work that can be innovative and able to make a 'trend'."

Or the problem is addressed to labor costs and inadequate salary

© 2018 OAXIES® LTD

Spa Manager at Therasia Resort Sea & Spa: "In Italy people are hiring only if the pay is on average because the labor cost is so high that an entrepreneur or a company before hiring a real professional think about that twice, so there is the search for a professional on average to play the role even if without talent or ability."

and

President of AISA: "The sector is growing, but still left to improvisation, so profits do not match expectations ... and wages are not adequate."

Or still underlining the lack of recognition to the role

Trainer & General Manager at Comfort Zone: "Many national entrepreneurs, unlike foreign colleagues, still have a lack of familiarity with the role: they often take on inadequate figures, lacking requisites, only with a beautician's experience, not even proven."

or

Chairman of CIDESCO Italia: "It is not very competitive, as the importance of this figure in the Italian spas is not yet completely clear."

This was later clarified when identifying the barriers and opportunities of the Italian Spa industry in relation to recruiting effective, competent and talented spa managers. Costs for labor, high salary and lack of investments has been recognised as the most important barriers.

Spa Manager at Mirtillo Rosso Family Hotel: "The barriers could be that the properties of the spas or hotels are almost never competent in wellness, they do not know exactly what the needs of the spa are and consequently they can not evaluate a suitable profile. The spa is often the last department on which invest, but they all clearly want it to be productive…"

and

Spa Manager at Gritti Palace Hotel: "As I already mentioned, I think that one of the brakes is a question of costs, we always try to save, but a competent and talented spa manager is able to form an excellent team, with which to achieve the required objectives, is able to understand in advance how the market moves and therefore knows how to make the right choices."

and

Spa Manager at Therasia Resort Sea & Spa: "The labor cost and the salary requested by the candidate."

and

President of AISA: "Costs precisely."

and

Chairman of CIDESCO Italia: "The high compensation rightly requested by the talented spa managers ... Only the spas with a certain turnover are able to hire competent and effective managers."

Lately, regarding the type of improvement in the Italian spa manager educational and training path the most emerged one was the implementation of an internship

Spa Manager at Gritti Palace Hotel : "I would give more weight to the part on the field, with longer internships."

and

Spa Manager at Mirtillo Rosso Family Hotel: "I would create a more detailed path alternating with internships, shadowing big

© 2018 OAXIES® LTD

spa managers."

and

Spa Manager at Therasia Resort Sea & Spa: "Paid internship on the field awarded by certificate from the company."

and

Trainer & General Manager at Comfort Zone: "A mandatory internship of 12 months…"

and

Spa Manager at H10 Hotels Roma: "Undertake an internship period in spas."

Or the enlargement and adaptation of programs, more structured and detailed

Wellness Consultant Self-employed at CJ Advisor Wellness & Sport: "To develop an academic competitive programme and to improve the spa industry itself in Italy (Wellness is not yet a trend in Italy like it is in other countries in EU) Austria is a forerunner in wellness. Presently many spa's in Italy running their spa without a Manager (small spa's are very often managed by therapists)."

and

Spa Manager at Hotel Terme Venezia Abano Terme: "Much more severity in vocational schools: to date, most of the professionals who leave the schools do not have a minimum competence in economics, marketing, strategy … None! Still much ignorance."

and

Spa Director at Hotel Milano Alpen Spa: "I would improve programs that offer a good general knowledge by adding management, CRM and marketing seminars."

and

Director of Spa & Soft Medical Operations at Terme di Saturnia: "High-profile management skills such as strategic and financial development in the company."

Or again underlining the need for role recognition

President of AISA: "The figure is missing, we need recognition."

and

Spa Manager at Dolce Vita Hotel Preidlhof : "The recognition in general can help to improve…".

4.4 DISCUSSION

In this section the key findings identified, that have been treated individually, are compared across the cases studied and using the analytical framework and key lines emerging from the literature, have been recombined.

Bearing in mind the primarily aims of this study is to investigate the effectiveness of professional training for the spa manager role in Italy, taking into account current educational system and programs, the line of inquiry for each case study was focused on: analysing the current training and educational systems programmes worldwide and in Italy, as effective routes to spa managerial positions and employment; analysing the skills and attributes required to operates as a spa manager in Italy and at international level; analysing the competitiveness, barriers and opportunities of the Italian spa industry in relation to recruiting effective, competent and talented spa managers; give recommen-

© 2018 OAXIES® LTD

dations for improving and implementing the Italian spa management educational and training system.

The analysis highlighted that the career for the most totality of interviewed has been in hospitality or in the beauty industry and for a minority in the fitness & wellness industry because, as stated by Rossi (2015) the work experience in hotels, in departments such as front office or public relations, can be helpful to facilitates the relationship with other departments and customers as well (Rossi, 2015). While the training undertaken has been mainly in beauty and complimentary therapy or academic degree plus some specialisation courses.

Confirming the survey conducted for the Global Spa & Wellness Summit (GSWS, 2012) stating that the industry relevance to educational qualifications when recruiting managers is little because the working experience in the management and spa sector is most important professional qualifications, followed by the importance of training or experience in spa, the experience has been deemed more important than education and training but has been difficult to determine the minimum amount of years needed.

According to Minardi (2017) a spa manager must be able to lead a group, being recognised as a leader and the analysis revealed leadership is the most important expected skill when hiring a spa manager, as well as operations management. Again, confirming Bielanski et al., human resources, marketing, finance, revenue management, IT and communication skills are the most important skills required for a spa manager role.

Moreover, a Beautician Vocational Qualification and Academic Degree are considered useful but not necessary an the ideal educational and training path suggested, in the absence of a specific path, is an academic degree in management or business and economic degree plus specialisation courses in the spa and wellness field, in agreement with the research conducted by Bielanski et al. (2011) claiming that most of the managers had a higher education, masters degree, bachelor's degree and a higher vocational education. Interestingly, the majority of interviewed is unaware of training and educational system in other countries but demonstrated dissatisfaction for the Italian spa manager educational and training system, suggesting as improvement the implementation of an internship and the recognition of the role, that clearly creates a gap in the training development. Moreover, it is interesting to note the willingness from representatives of trade associations and training associations to improve and work on a new educational and training system, hand in hand with the adaptation of regulations. It is interesting to note that the majority of interviewed, despite working within the industry, is unaware of Italian regulations and laws; while others recognises their obsolescence as barriers for the development of education and training. Furthermore, the labor costs and high salary of managers has been recognised as the main barrier for the Italian spa industry competitiveness as well as the lack of recognition of the figure both in the educational and professional sector.

© 2018 OAXIES® LTD

5 CONCLUSIONS AND RECOMMENDATIONS

Concluding, based on the key findings there is the need in Italy for a specific path for spa management educational programmes. Indeed, as stated by Global Spa and Wellness Summit (2012), nowadays there are only a fews and the existing ones are seen as weak in preparing students for the workplace. The gaps in the Italian education and training system for spa management that must be overcome, identified as barriers for its development, are the obsolescence of Italian regulations and laws, in particular Italian Law Reordering the Thermal Spa Sector Law no. 323/2000 and Discipline of the Beautician Activity Law no. 1/1990, but there is the willingness from representatives of trade associations and training associations, aware of the need to change and expand the law in order to make changes, on working on it to improve the current spa management educational and training system, hand in hand with the change and adaptation of regulations.

Also, the costs for labor, the high salary for managers and lack of investments in the sector has been recognised as the most important barriers.

Despite most respondents are unaware of the education and training system in other countries, also representatives of training and trade associations, the current status of Italian training and educational systems for spa manager has been described unsatisfactory, superficial, defective and incomplete.

Moreover, the interviewed could not recognise a benchmarking or competitiveness of Italian spa management educational system but only dissatisfaction and backwardness, pointing out both the lack and the need of recognition of the role, at educational and profession level, and of a specific spa management path, which clearly create a gap in the system.

Solutions and suggestions for improvement have been identified in the enlargement and adaptation of existing programmes, more structured and detailed with focus on marketing, business and human resources; and the implementation of an internship in the spa environment to learn the job.

This study extends the body of knowledge on the Italian educational and training system for spa manager, highlighting the gaps for its development and suggesting possible solutions.

Nevertheless, limitations to this research derive from the impossibility of being able to interview more trainers and representatives of trade associations and training associations, who could have been explained more in detail the situation. Furthermore, the impossibility of carrying out interviews to some instead of questionnaires, to investigate the problem more deeply.

Suggestions for academia and for future research includes the possibility of including a quantitative study to better understand the complex status of the educational and training system in Italy, which can help avoid bias.

© 2018 OAXIES® LTD

BIBLIOGRAPHY

AICEB (2010). *Il mercato del benessere: imprese e servizi offerti.* Rimini, 14 maggio.

Altman, N. (2000). *Healing Springs: The Ultimate Guide to Taking the Waters - From Hidden Springs to the World's Greatest Spas.* Rochester, Vermont: Healing Arts Press.

Australian Qualification Framework AQF (2018). Available at: https://www.aqf.edu.au/ [Accessed on 10th April 2018].

Baker, T.L. (1994). *Doing Social research (2nd Edn.).* New York: McGraw-Hill Inc.

Becheri, E. And Quirino, N. (2011). *Il benessere termale in Italia, in E. Becheri and G. Maggiore (eds) Rapporto sul turismo italiano 2010-2012.* Milano: Franco Angeli, pp. 427-43.

Becheri, E. & Quirino, N. (2012). *Rapporto sul Sistema Termale in Italia 2012.* Italy, FrancoAngeli.

Bielański, M., Saari, S., Wilkońska, A., Tuominen, T., Mora, I., Binder, D., Adamski, P. (2011). *Challenges for the European SPA Management. Results of the ILIS Project. Polish Journal of Sport and Tourism*, 18(2).

Bryman, A., (2015). *Social Research Methods.* Oxford, Oxford University Press.

Buxton, L. (2017). *Thermal and Mineral Springs. In S. Raw-*

linson & T. Heap (Eds.), International Spa Management: Principles and practice (pp. 23-35). Oxford: Goodfellow Publishers Ltd.

Casillas, J.C, Acedo F. J. and Barbero J. L. (2010). *Learning, unlearning and internationalisation: Evidence from the pre-export phase International Journal of Information*, 30(2) 162-173.

City and Guilds (2018). Available at: www.city-and-guilds.co.uk [Accessed on 10th April 2018].

Cohen, M. and G. Bodeker (2008). *Understanding the Global Spa Industry: Spa Management.* London: Butterworth & Heinemann.

Comité International d'Esthétique et de Cosmétologie CIDESCO (2018). Available at: www.cidesco.com [Accessed on 10th April 2018].

Commission on Massage Therapy Accreditation CMTA (2018) Available at: https://comta.org/ [Accessed on 10th April 2018].

Corbin, J., Strauss, A. (2008). *Basics of Qualitative Research.* London, SAGE.

Crang, M., Cook, I. (2007). *Doing Ethnographies.* London, SAGE.

Creswell, J. (2013). *Research design: qualitative, quantitative, and mixed- method approaches.* Los Angeles, SAGE.

Crotty, M. (1998). *The foundations of social research: meaning and perspective in the research process.* London, SAGE.

Denzin N., Lincoln. Y. (2013). *Collecting and interpreting qualitative materials.* Thousand Oaks, SAGE.

Denzin, N., Lincoln, Y. (2013). *The landscape of qualitative*

© 2018 OAXIES® LTD

research. Los Angeles, SAGE.

Ecipar Bologna (2018). Available at: https://eciparbologna.it/ [Accessed on 10th April 2018].

Enaip Veneto Available at: http://www.enaip.veneto.it/ [Accessed on 10th April 2018].

European Spa Association ESPA (2018). Available at: http://www.espa-ehv.eu/ [Accessed on 10th April 2018].

Faroldi, E., Cipullo, F. And Vettori, M. P. (2007). *Terme e architettura. Progetti, tecnologie, strategie per una moderna cultura termale.* Bologna: Maggioli.

Federation of State Massage Therapy Boards FSMTB (2018). Available at: http://www.fsmtb.org/www.fsmtb.org [Accessed on 10th April 2018].

Ferrari, S. (2014). *Italian spas today: Demand and offer evolution and trends.* In Smith, M. And Puczó, L. (Eds.), Health, Tourism and Hospitality: Spas, wellness and medical travel. (pp. 259-263). London: Routledge.

Foster, L. T. and Keller, C. P. (2008). *British Columbia Atlas of Wellness.* Available at: at http://www.geog.uvic.ca/wellness/ [Accessed on 10th April 2018].

Frost, G. J. (2004). *The spa as a model of an optimal healing environment. The Journal of Alternative and Complementary Medicine,* 10(1), 85-92.

Gazzetta Ufficiale della Repubblica Italiana (2000). *Legge 24 ottobre 2000, n. 323: Riordino del settore termale.* Available at: http://www.gazzettaufficiale.it/eli/id/2000/11/08/000G0377/sg [Accessed on 10th April 2018].

Gazzetta Ufficiale della Repubblica Italiana (2018). *Decre-*

to 15 ottobre 2015, n. 206. Available at: http://www.gazzettauffi-ciale.it/eli/id/2015/12/28/15G00218/sg [Accessed on 10th April 2018].

Global Wellness Institute GWI (2014). *Global Spa & Wellness Economy Monitor, prepared by SRI International.*

Global Spa & Wellness Summit GSWS (2012). *Spa Management Workforce and Education: Addressing Market Gaps.* [Online] United States, SRI International. Available at http://www.globalspaandwellnesssummit.org/images/stories/pdf/gsws.2012.research.spa.management.workforce.education.re-vised.june.2012.pdf [Accessed 18th March 2018].

Gratton, C., Jones, I. (2004). *Research methods for sports studies.* London, Routledge Taylor & Francis.
Gray, D. (2014). *Doing research in the real world.* Los Angeles, SAGE.

Gutenbrunner, C., Bender, T., Cantista, P. And Karagulle, Z. (2010). A *proposal for a worldwide definition of health resort medicine, balneology, medical hydrology and climatology,* International Journal of Biometeorology, 54, 495-597.

Hair And Beauty Industry Authority HABIA (2018). Available at: www.habia.org.uk [Accessed on 10th April 2018].

International Union of Tourism Organisations IUTO (1973). Health Tourism. Geneva: United Nations.

International Spa Association ISPA (2017). *Global Best Practices.* Available at: https://experienceispa.com/images/pdfs/Global-Best-Practices_2017Updates.pdf [Accessed on 10th April 2018].

International Spa Association ISPA (2018). Available at: https://experienceispa.com/resources/spa-goers [Accessed on 10th April 2018].

   © 2018 OAXIES® LTD

Istituti Tecnici Superiori (2018). *Sistema ITS*. Available at: http://www.sistemaits.it/ [Accessed on 10th April 2018].

Italian National Statistical Institute ISTAT (2008). *The Wellness Sector in Italy*. ISTAT.

La Legge per Tutti (2018). *La Disciplina dell'Attività di Estetista*. Available at: https://www.laleggepertutti.it/176174_la-disciplina-dellattivita-di-estetista [Accessed on 10th April 2018].

LUISS Business School (2018). *Master in Management della Filiera della Salute - Major in Management delle Aziende Sanitarie*. Available at: http://businessschool.luiss.it/management-aziende-sanitarie/ [Accessed on 10th April 2018].

Massage Therapy Association of South Africa MTASA (2018). Available at: http://mtasa.co.za/ [Accessed on 10th April 2018].

Minardi R. (2017). *Spa: da centro di costo a centro di ricavo*. Il Nuovo Club. 153(27), 54-58.

Minichiello, V. (1991). *In-depth interviewing: Researching people*. Melbourne: Longman Cheshire.

Ministero della Salute (2018). *Decreto Legislativo 04 agosto 2016, n. 171*. Available at: http://www.trovanorme.salute.gov.it/norme/dettaglioAtto?id=55791&articolo=1 [Accessed on 10th April 2018].

Ministero dello Sviluppo Economico (2018). *Legge 4 gennaio 1990, n. 1. Disciplina dell'attività di estetista*. Available at: http://www.sviluppoeconomico.gov.it/images/stories/normativa/legge1_1990-attivita-estetista.pdf [Accessed on 10th April 2018].

National Certification Board for Therapeutic Massage & Bodywork NCBTMB (2018). Available at: www.ncbtmb.com [Accessed on 10th April 2018].

Opera Armida Barelli (2018). Available at: http://site.operaar-midabarelli.org [Accessed on 10th April 2018].

Potter, J. (1996). *Discourse analysis and constructionist approaches: theoretical background.* In: Richardson, J., (ed.), Handbook of Qualitative Research Methods for Psychology and the Social Sciences, Leicester, British Psychological Society, pp. 125-140.

Potter, J. (2012). *Discourse analysis and discursive psychology.* In: Cooper, H., (ed.), APA Handbook of Research Methods in Psychology, Washington, American Psychological Association Press, Vol. 2, pp. 111-130.

Regione Emilia Romagna (2018). *Formazione e Lavoro.* Available at: http://formazionelavoro.regione.emilia-romagna.it/formazione-regolamentata/estetista#formazione-regolamenta-ta-b--nbsp---b- [Accessed on 10th April 2018].

Rawlinson, S. and Heap, T. (2017). *International Spa Management: Principles and practice.* UK: Goodfellow Publishers Limited.

Rawlinson, S. (2017). *The Evolution of Spa.* In S. Rawlinson & T. Heap (Eds.), International Spa Management: Principles and practice (pp. 1-13). Oxford: Goodfellow Publishers Ltd.

Rossi, G. (2015). *Lavori da Sogno: Come Sono Diventata Spa Manager. Cosmopolitan.* Available at: http://www.cosmopolitan.it/lifecoach/lavoro-carriera/how-to/a111085/lavori-da-sogno-spa- manager/ [Accessed on 10th April 2018].

Saunders, M., Lewis, P., Thornhill, A. (2009). R*esearch Methods for Business Students, (4thEd).* Harlow, FT Prentic.

Silverman, D. (2016). Qualitative research. Los Angeles,

 © 2018 OAXIES® LTD

SAGE.

Smith, M. And Kelly, C. (2006). *Wellness Tourism. Tourism Recreation Research,* 31 (1), 1-4.

Smith, M. And Puczó, L. (2014). *Health, Tourism and Hospitality: Spas, wellness and medical travel.* London: Routledge.

The Allied Health Professions Council of South Africa AHPCSA (2018). Available at: www.ahpcsa.co.za [Accessed on 10th April 2018].

The Confederation of International Beauty Therapy and Cosmetology CIBTAC (2018). Available at: www.cibtac.com [Accessed on 10th April 2018].

The International Spa Association ISPA (2018). Spa-Goers. Available at: https://experienceispa.com/resources/spa-goers [Accessed on 10th April 2018].

The International Therapy Examination Council ITEC (2018). Available at: www.itecworld.co.uk [Accessed on 10th April 2018].

Thomas, G. (2011). *How to do your case study.* London, SAGE.

Van Teijlingen E. R. and Hundley V. (2001). *The Importance of Pilot Study, Social Research Update,* Number 35, Department of Sociology University of Surrey Available at: http://aura.abdn.ac.uk/bitstream/handle/2164/157/SRU35%20pilot%20studies.pdf?sequence=1&isAllowed=y [Accessed on 10th April 2018].
Veal, A. (2011). *Research methods for leisure and tourism.* Harlow, Financial Times Prentice Hall.

Veal, A., Burton, C. (2014). *Research Methods for arts and event management.* Harlow, Pearson Education Limited.

Vocational Training Charitable Trust VTCT (2018). Available at: http://www.vtct.org.uk [Accessed on 10th April 2018].

Virgintino, D. & Bovero, B. (2013). *Spa Management: Scegliere, gestire, lavorare nel benessere.* Italy, Tecniche Nuove.

Yin, R. (2009). *Case study research: design and methods.* London, SAGE.

© 2018 OAXIES® LTD

NOTES

NOTES

© 2018 OAXIES® LTD

NOTES

© 2018 OAXIES® LTD

NOTES

© 2018 OAXIES® LTD

NOTES

NOTES

© 2018 OAXIES® LTD

NOTES

© 2018 OAXIES® LTD

NOTES

© 2018 OAXIES® LTD

NOTES

NOTES

© 2018 OAXIES® LTD

NOTES

NOTES

© 2018 OAXIES® LTD

NOTES

© 2018 OAXIES® LTD

NOTES

© 2018 OAXIES® LTD

NOTES

NOTES

© 2018 OAXIES® LTD

NOTES

NOTES

© 2018 OAXIES® LTD

NOTES

© 2018 OAXIES® LTD

NOTES

© 2018 OAXIES® LTD

NOTES